My Badass Mouth

self-help

Lemuel Maranan

Published by Lemuel Maranan

Text Copyright© 2020 Lemuel Maranan
Illustration Copyright© 2020 Lemuel Maranan
Book Layout by Donna Burke

All rights reserved. No part of this book may be reproduced or transmitted in any form or by any means, electronic or mechanical, including photocopying, recording or by any information storage and retrieval system, without written permission of the publisher, except for inclusion of brief quotations in a review.

Printed in the United States of America

ISBN: 978-1-7351456-0-0

Back Cover Photo: Grace Antonio, Justin Peralta, and Rollybeth Sagayap

ABUSE

Abuse doesn't care. It does its intention
if it sees a chance and only applies
if tolerates... a burden.

ACTION

Let action not be an injury.
With responsible actions,
you will avoid trouble.

If your action affects others,
you cannot say,
"It's none of your business."

ADDICTION

It starts with curiosity and
ends up in addiction.

Addiction is slavery,
freedom is victory.

ANGER

Anger exposes secrets.
Anger can make the educated wild.
Anger might darken your mind, yet it may lighten other.
An angry confrontation is like pouring gasoline
onto a small fire.

ANT

If an ant is given the strength
of a beetle and its action cannot hide
it, then it may perceive wrongly as
arrogance by both some ant and beetle.

ARGUMENT

Arguments are nonsense.
Arguments have no winner; both parties think they're right.

ARROGANCE

The fruit of arrogance is disorder.
Pray that the received strength will not turn into pride.
The outcome of arrogance is failure and shame.
Those who are proud and walk with pride will surely be humiliated.

ATTITUDE

Attitude can be the
problem solver or
the very cause of the
problem.

BAD CHOICE

Narrow minded, close minded,
and stubbornness are not different.
All are, "it's all about me", concept...
It's a choice - a bad choice.

BATTLE

Without battle there is no victory.
Sometimes you need to stop fighting in
order to win the battle... just humble yourself.
Be aware, there are battles where fighting
will be counted as a loss.

TWO KINDS OF BATTLE

The worth fighting for.
The toxic fight.
Choose your battle wisely.

BEAUTY

The downfall of beauty makes the character reign.
Beauty is less appreciated if it's common.
The beauty of the mind starts when young,
and it blooms when you are old.

BE HEALED

What people need is to be healed from the wounds of the past; for if not, he'll be miserable all the days of his life even if he is already prosperous.

BETTER

It's better to be treated as an enemy of your weakness than befriend it and fall.

Better not to tell others your dream; they may just tell you you're ambitious.

It's better to stop battling to change somebody. Why not do the change yourself? You might influence them.

It's better to be homeless than to be hopeless.

It's better not to talk about your failure; they'll just put the blame on you.

Tiredness is much better then boredom.

Obeying is much better than teaching.

Better to be content with memory.

Portrait may just cause sorrow and home sick in a distant land.

BE WISE

Be wise in your step; there are temporary satisfactions that may lead to destruction.

Be wise when you prosper.
Lazy people await.

BITTERNESS

Forgiving and forgetting do not make you bitter.
Forgiving and forgetting make you better.

Let go of the grudge, the thing that torments you everyday.

BLESSINGS IN DISGUISE

The storm will make you strong and the problem will make you wise. These two are blessings in disguise.

BOREDOM

Boredom can cause unreasonable expenses and insane things.
Boredom pushes the lazy to move.
Boredom is not that you do not do anything, but the result of repetition.

Life without purpose is boring.

BRAVE AND COWARD

The brave faces his fear.
The coward is content with his situation.
Only the brave can speak boldly of the truth.

The coward hates obligation... that's why the only option is to run away from it.

BULLYING

Bullying is insecurity. It is the result of longing for attention, recognition, and acceptance. It is cowardice, for its prey is weaker.

CAGE

If you don't get out,
you remain in your cage.

It's your decision.
Jesus is the way,
the answer, and the solution.

CAPTURE THE HEART

When you captured the eyes, you just captured the attention. But when you captured the heart, you captured everything.

CATCH

The catch will always depend on the bait.
If you catch nothing, change the bait.

CHANCE

Chance may be the solution.

As long as a man is breathing, he has a chance for a new beginning.

Change is a door of chance, and chance is a door of possibilities.

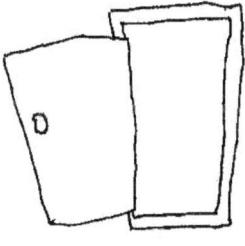

CHANGE

Willingness with cooperation will result in changes.

Confessing wrong deeds is a sign of intelligence. It is the biggest chance for change.

Change is a beautiful thing. But going there is very rough, and only the tough gets there.
Use your condition as an inspiration to change your situation.
In order to change the situation, why not do the change first and things may follow.

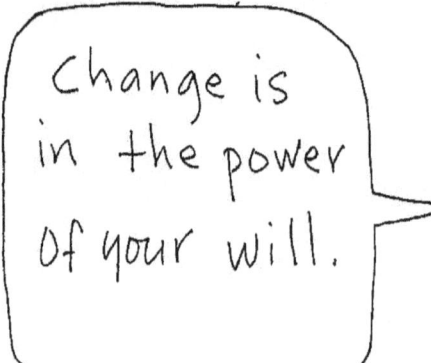

Change is in the power of your will.

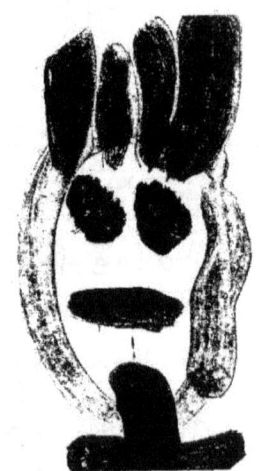

CHILD

The children are the reflection of their parents.

What you sowed to your parents, you will reap from your children.

A baby is just borrowed from God.
Be careful how you treat a child, for while you are getting weaker they are getting stronger.

COMPANION

Bearing others characters and not others bearing yours results in good companions.
Happiness is not in the place; it is in your companion.

CONFIDENCE

A confident man doesn't care too much
about what he is wearing.
If your confidence is with the crowd,
then you're weak when alone.

Confidence is influence, and influence is power.

CONSIDERATION

Consideration is expensive, for
not everybody can afford it.
But if you give it freely,
people will find you exceptional.

CONVERSATION

A good conversation does not require a good speaker;
it requires a good listener.

Conversation is like water that sustains the plant. It sustains the relationship.

COUNSEL

Counsel is ignored until it's proven to be true.

Counsel is like medicine; tastes bitter,
but effective if taken.

COURAGE

If you have too much courage,
you'd have too many enemies.

Facing and challenging things
beyond your capacity is bravery.

CRAVING

Avoid looking on longing, it only boosts craving.

The thing you crave for is the thing you envy.

Craving is not in the absence
of what you long for.
It's in the presence.

CRITICISM

Covering up criticism is a sign of immaturity.

Criticism results in betterment if taken positively.

DECISION

Bad decision teaches to move wisely.
When people finish things, it might be their final decision.

DEFEAT

> CONSIDERATION DEFEATS SELFISHNESS.
> SATISFACTION DEFEATS ENVY.
> CONTENTMENT DEFEATS BOREDOM.
> TRUST DEFEATS WORRIES.
> PEACE DEFEATS SORROWS.
> WISDOM DEFEATS CIRCUMSTANCES.
> UNDERSTANDING DEFEATS ANGER.
> FORGIVENESS DEFEATS RESENTMENT, HATRED, AND BITTERNESS.
> HOPE DEFEATS DARKNESS.

DESIRE

> Your desire determines your destiny.
>
> Desire improvement.

DISCIPLINE

The good ingredient for diligence is discipline.
Discipline is like a strict mother that guides
you for betterment.
Let discipline rule yourself.
Discipline is like a beautiful crown that is being
displayed without you knowing it.
Lack of discipline ruins life.
Discipline yourself, and you will be a conqueror.
Discipline your tongue, and you will be a great
conqueror.
Love disciplines... it's harsh.

DISCRIMINATION

Discrimination is like saying, "you are nothing."
Discrimination is not different from oppression.
There's a good and a bad discrimination. The good is
when you do not do what the bad do.

DO NOT

Do not pay too much attention to your weakness. It will weaken your willpower.

Do not be proud to the customer in time of progress. They brought you up there.

Do not pay attention to a hotheaded person. Instead of him feeling remorse alone, it could be the both of you.

Do not forget the cycle of life - that the baby will come back to a baby. And when it happens, it requires double patience.

Do not entertain negative words; it's the enemy of willpower.

Don't use your freedom to be enslaved - to be enslaved by evil desires.

Don't treat small things as a small thing, but the beginning of big things.

Do not fear bad guys, and they will respect you.

Do not take for granted the person who watched and nursed you now that you are a grown-up.

Do not chase the kind of wealth that could corrupt you.

Do not be troubled by those people who show opposition against you. As long as you're not doing wrong, that is what matters.

Do not get beyond somebody's limitation or taste their worst part.

Do not be cranky when facing a problem or you worsen it.

Do not display your greediness in public or you bring disgrace to yourself.

Do not pamper a crybaby or you help him to be a weak person.

Do not play worse than the owner at work or you make trouble.

Do not let emotion dictate action in a bad condition, it may result a regretful decision.

DO NOT BE DISMAYED

Do not be dismayed if your life is too slow. Remember, Noah's Ark didn't close until the snail got in.

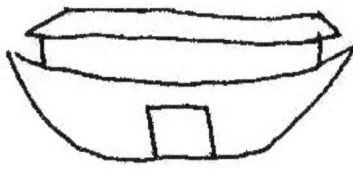

DON'T GIVE UP

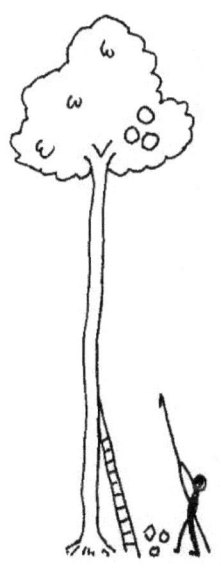

A man is trying to get a fruit on a tree, but his stick can't reach it. He uses a ladder, but still, the tree is tall. He shakes the tree, but the tree is steady. He throws a stone, but the branch is thick. When he is about to surrender, the wind blows, and the fruit falls.

You never know what may come next.

Don't give up.

DREAM

Do not just dream a house... dream a home.

A Dream that destroys home is not a dream, but a nightmare.

Man's dreams push him to endeavor.

Dream without work is just a fantasy.

The dream is very far from reality, but in reality, you start your dream.

A dream is fun to a lone person; for there he finds company.

Dream is a disease that only fulfillment can cure.

IF you want your dream to be fruitful, step away from your sleeping.

DRUGS

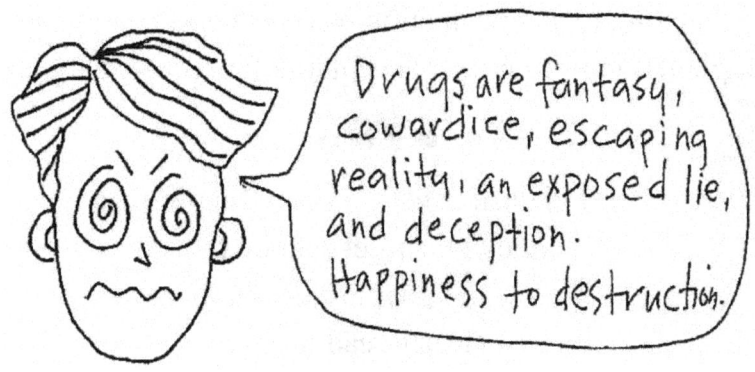

EDUCATION

Education kills extreme poverty.

The resource is not the main problem
of the poorest, but the education to create it.

EXPECTATION

Pain is the result of frustration.
Frustration is the result of expectation.
Whether doing good for people
or doing nothing, expect nothing...
Avoid frustration - avoid pain.
Too much closeness, too much expectation.
If you do not meet expectation,
it results in separation with anger.

EXPLANATION

Listening to an explanation results in good company.
Explanation is no longer acceptable for repeated actions.

EYES

Eyes and desires have a common problem;
they never get satisfied.
The eyes of old people can clearly read -
clearly read life.

Eyes, the judgmental.

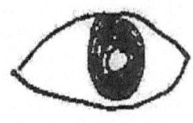

FAITHFUL

The faithful will never lack anything.
The faithful are like a big rock in a rushing river.
Cannot be moved, and cannot be carried away. Steady

FAMILY

When you create a family, it's not all about you anymore.

Family is the precious thing next to God.

Focus

Focus on Jesus not on the trials.

Focus on your strength not on your weakness.

Focus on the future not on the past.

Focus on the good result not on the struggle.
Focus

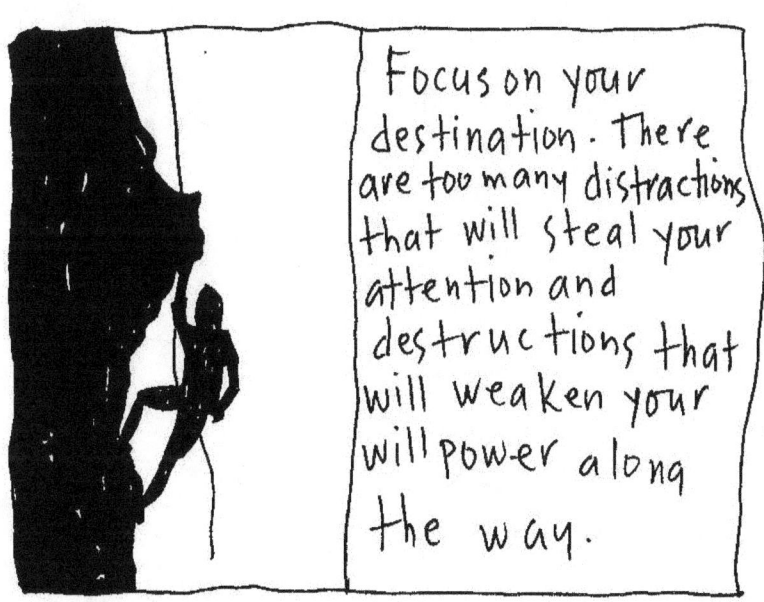

Focus on your destination. There are too many distractions that will steal your attention and destructions that will weaken your willpower along the way.

Remember: People will use your past as a tool to fail you. Be focused.

FORGIVENESS

Forgiveness is the antidote to all bitterness.
Forgiveness applies to all, not just to the select.
Only forgiveness heals a wounded heart,
and only understanding makes forgiveness easy.
Forgiveness restores and mercy covers all.

Forgiveness is like sugar that sweetens the bitter coffee. It sweetens the bitter relationship.

You will never learn to forget until you learn to forgive.

FRIENDSHIP

A Friend can never be an enemy forever.

Sometimes, enemies become good friends.

Be careful with your best friend, he could be your worst enemy.

Sometimes, a fight becomes a way to friendship.

The wrong friends give joy and fun -
joy and fun that lead to destruction.

GAMBLING

Gambling is like a fire that will consume your possessions in a matter of time.

A gambler will end up broke.

GUILT

Being free from any guilt is like being free from any burden.

Feeling guilt means changes.

HARDSHIP

If hardship becomes your way of life,
it's not that hard anymore.

The hardship of life will bring out the best in you.

Hardship builds character. It's either better
or bitter.

HATE

To lead is to direct and gain haters.

Execute the right by exposing the wrong and you will be hated.

HELP

You don't just help, but also teach. For help is consumed, but lessons last.

Mercy is for those who want to help themselves.

If possible, offer help without blaming, but with only encouragement.

Help is the instinct of a good man.

When asking for help, do not use curse words or you may lose sympathy.

HONOR

the strong should face the stronger not the weak in order to get honor.

HOT-HEADED

A hot-headed person is like an explosive.
When it explodes it destroys...
including himself.

HUMILITY

What is humility? It is the ability
to control and hold arrogance.

Humility is a sign of maturity.

Humility means to treat the humble fairly.

Learning humility may seem false at first,
but practice makes perfect.

HUMOR

A touch of humor makes the conversation
comfortable.

Nonsense becomes sensible when it is put to humor or
sense of humor.

HYPOCRISY

When you go to church do not focus your
attention on the people for you might just see
hypocrisy. Neither should people look at you.

INFORM

Poor man, you are not in a position to waste your life.
Wake up.

Lazy man, you set goals.
Goals can motivate you to move.

Intelligent people, anything you do wrong
in your knowledge is stupid.

INSECURITY

Selflessness overcomes insecurity.

People who always find fault to prove they are better
than you are insecure. Ignore them,
they are a waste of time.

INTELLIGENCE

A wise man never spends time thinking about the problem. But only about the solution.

A Wise man knows when to shut up and when to talk.

A wise man marks everything that failed him and never does it again.

The intelligence that can never be used in livelihood is useless.

Who plays dumb well? The intellectual.

One word is enough for an intelligent man.

A wise man never lets feelings rule judgment.

A wise man chooses humility over his ego in order to win favor.

A wise man frees himself from hate,
for it benefits him nothing.
Just a burden to mind and heart

JEALOUSY

Jealousy doesn't see appearance; it's all about attention.

Too much love begets too much jealousy.

Jealousy brings hatred to loved ones, especially to close loved ones.

Jealousy results in slander and insult.

When Jealousy comes in, hatred follows.

Jealousy adds spice to a relationship; but if you do it regularly it becomes vinegar that makes the relationship sour.

Envy can result in hatred or inspiration.

JESUS CHRIST

Jesus Christ is the missing puzzle piece.

Too many questions... Jesus Christ is the answer. Nothing else.

KINDNESS

Kindness is not dumbness. It is intelligence, for it does what is right. It is free will, but has boundaries.
Kindness is just an investment for the unkind to get their interests.
Sometimes, being kind is exhausting, but to be bad is fearsome.

LEADERSHIP

Rules will not be obeyed if the executive is a violator.

A good leader is a good follower.

LIFE

Life is not live to eat, but eat to live.
Life is like money. Spend it wisely.
Life is a never-ending process of learning.
Life on earth is only an experience.
Life is like a sport. Loosing requires a change of the game plan.
Life is not a life without a problem or trial. It's a part of being alive.
Life is too short and the one who enjoys it the most is the one who's just living for himself.

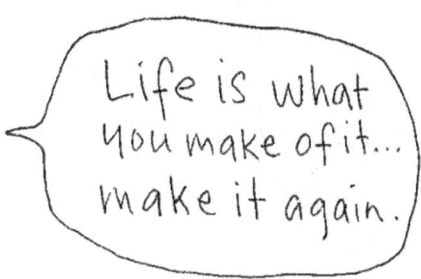

Life is what you make of it... make it again.

LIGHT AND DARKNESS

Light gives things color. Darkness shows men's true colors.

Light gives friends. Darkness gives true friends.

LOVE

Money is better than beauty, but love conquers all.

Love is a sense of feeling and not a sense of seeing.

Love requires a strong heart and a broad mind.

Love is neither a word nor a written word. It is an action.

Love always gives reasons.

Love means acceptance without judgment.

Love must shine more at the worst time.

Love is a package deal.

When love is greater than lust, love will last.

You may never find love if you do not give it first.

MANAGEMENT

Discipline and management are like a husband and a wife; they work together.

Time management accomplishes things.

MAN AND WOMAN

Man is usually stronger than a woman, but often he gets strength from a woman.

Man is tougher than a woman, but in reality, he's weaker when it comes to love.

MANIPULATION

Manipulation uses its contribution to control things, but the wise rejects it right away. (Use good sense)

Manipulation is not different from bullying; both start trouble.

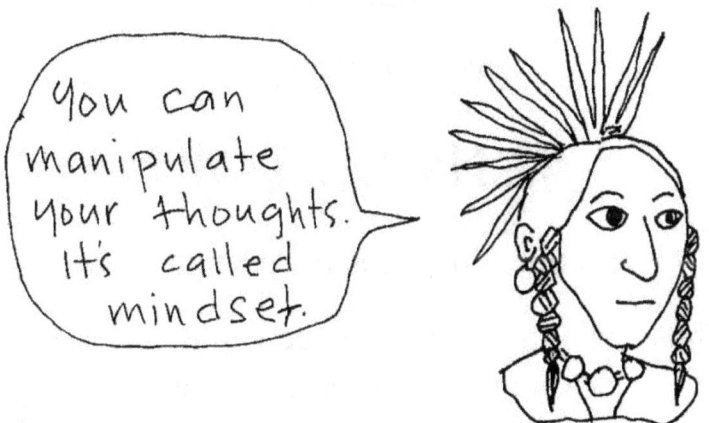

MANNER

Achieving good manners is the only success you could bring after death.

The basis for respect is not education, not even life's circumstances. It's all about manners. Good manners.

What are good table manners if your attitude is bad?

The real manners of a person can be found inside his house.

MIND

In some cases, it is the mind that needs to be fixed, and not the situation or anything.

Mind over matter doesn't change anything... but still, it helps.

It's all in the mind.

MISTREATMENT

Mistreatment happens if it's being allowed.

Those who mistreat others defend themselves by calling the mistreated sensitive.

MORE SENSIBLE

Who's more sensible, the savage who knows that there is a higher authority who controls everything or the civilized atheist who's out of their own knowledge denying the existence of the
Most High **GOD?**

NEVER

Never go for illegal thing; it is only a short-term comfort.

Never play and trust danger. It is tricky and a traitor.

Never long for anyone, for they voluntarily come when you already have money.

Never satisfy your anger at work or you get fired.

NO BOUNDARY

One of the reason why some family members cannot get along with each other is because of having no boundary.

OBEDIENCE

Obedience offers no options.
The key to obedience is waiting.

PAST

Questioning the past will ruin the present.

Indulging the past is really stupid. It is like a fog that blocks your sight - your sight of the present and future.

> Keep recalling the past will just energize your frustration.
> It would not do any better on the present.
> It's either you punish yourself or move on.

PATIENCE

Patience can bear tiredness and boredom.
Patience will result strength and calmness.
Patience is beautiful,
but it turns ugly when it pushes the limit.

Even if you are the smartest and the most diligent worker, if you don't have patience, you will not last at work.

PERSONALITY

The personality of a person reflects his environment.

Personality lies on integrity.

Personality has its own proper place. There, it finds more effectiveness.

Nobody can destroy your personality, but you alone.

POSITIVE AND NEGATIVE

A positive person searches for beauty in the unpleasant. A negative one searches for the unpleasant in the beautiful.

PRAYERFUL

A prayerful person will defeat his enemy.

A man of prayer is a man of power.

PRETENSE

Pretense is a fear... fear of rejection.

Those who do not pretend are more liked and loved by the people.

A pretend greeting is like a gift that contains rotten food.

PRIDE

Pride is like a wall that divides a loving couple. It hides the love for each other. Destroy the wall. Destroy the pride. Expose the love.

> Pride can make you feel big, but it can also make you feel small.

PROBLEM

Problems never end. That's why old people are wise; they solved a lot of them.

The first thing to solve a problem is to face the problem.

Resolve a possible issue before it becomes a problem. The big problem always starts with a small problem... resolve the problem right away.

PROMISE

The promise of God keeps those who believe still.

Do not expect the promise of the person who is in need.

Promises are made to be broken by those who have no integrity.

PROMOTION

Promotion will expose what kind of person you are.

Promotion is just a test whether you deserve it or not.

PUNISH

> If you punish yourself by the guilt of the past and be scared of the unseen future, then your present will be filled with unhappiness and anxiety.

QUESTION

What is beauty without an admirer?

What is diligence if it will not result in progress?

Who is luckier, the young who's just starting to run or the old who's already resting?

What is the most precious gift you could give to your partner? Faithfulness.

If no one asks you to do it, Why complain?

Are we a solution or a problem?

Sit, talk, listen, and consider, why not?

Why waste time on the things you cannot change?

Are we inspiration or destruction?

If the person doesn't care about his offspring,
what about others?

What is strength without courage?

Why stress-out yourself from the things you cannot
change and has no answer?

Is there a wise man that never knows
whether he tells right or wrong?

REALITY

Reality: God displays His strength to the weak,
His wisdom to the fool.

Are you weak and foolish? Be of good cheer.

REALIZATION

Realization is a good compass. It shows where you are and where you're going. It pinpoints your mistakes and directs you to the right.

Realization is change.

REBUILDING YOURSELF

Forgive yourself
Forgive others
Ask for forgiveness
Three things to start rebuilding yourself.

REFRAIN

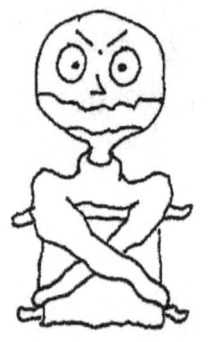

Refrain from moving, talking, and making decisions when you are angry. For no good thought is running in your mind at the moment.

REJECTION

Rejection may not be heard in words, but may clearly be seen in action. However, you can convert it into a strong motivation to change your condition.

REMORSE

Remorse is greater than mistake.

Deep loneliness means remorse.

REMOVE THE WORM

Marriage is like a plant and temptation is like the worm that eats and destroys the plant and the fruit. Entertaining temptation is like putting a worm in the plant... Protect the plant - protect the marriage.
Protect the fruit - your children...
remove the worm.

RESPECT

With the absence of respect, there is chaos.

> When there is respect, there is peace.

The more help you ask, the less respect you get.

He who desires respect should be the first to execute it.

Respect is a free thing. Share it equally.

RIGHT AND WRONG

You learn right from wrong.

Choosing right from wrong lies in the power of your will.

ROOT OF ALL WARS

Conflict in beliefs is the root of all wars. For what is good to one is bad to others. What is bad to one is good to others.

RUDENESS

Rudeness selects no one. It can be possessed by both the uneducated and the educated.

Rudeness is like stinky garbage that should be thrown away. But to them who exercise it, it's like a crown that should be displayed.

Being disrespectful will make you different from others. You will be marked as, "the rude one."

Paying no attention to a rude person shows only that you are of higher esteem.

RULES

Rules are the basic law of harmony.

Rules are made for the benefit of everybody.

RUN

A snail joined a race.
He was very slow, yet
he finished the race.
Pause, but never stop.
Slow as you are, still,
the finish line awaits.

SCAM

Be aware: Do not be too confident. Sometimes acquaintances scam you. Why? Because they know you trust them.

Do not be blinded by beauty and sweet words. It could only be a front for scam.

Laziness is the root of all scams.

SCAR

A Scar is evident that a wound is healed. If you are already okay and still look bad, that's the only scar.

SECRET

A secret is not a lie. It is not a sin. The people don't need to know everything about you. A life that is an open book can be a center of ridicule unless it is inspirational.

SELFISHNESS

The most unbearable kind of selfishness is the one that causes injury to others, yet doesn't care.

A selfish person prefers his things to rot than to give them to others.

SELF-PITY

Self-pity is a toxic thing. Its poison makes people bitter, ungrateful, and unappreciative of what they have. It weakens willpower and can paralyze people to move forward.
It is the worse form of jealousy that eats joy and confidence.

SILENCE

Silence speaks so loudly.

Silence can speak without doing anything.

Silence can keep you away from trouble.

Your silence may justify wrong and compromise.

SITUATION

Learn to sing in the midst of heat. Learn to hum when winter comes. Joy awaits those who persevere.
The situation is like a season.
It doesn't stay. It keeps changing for a reason.
Cheer up!

SMILE

A smile means you are welcome for a moment.

A smile is an open door for an aggressive person.

A smile is so simple, yet it makes you feel good as a person.

SOLITUDE

To be alone is to understand fully your purpose.

In your solitude, you will know your real companion...
It's Jesus Christ.

SOLUTION

Use your toughness in resolving the problem,
not being the cause.

SOMEHOW

Somehow, things are less valuable while existing.

Innocence is not bravery, but somehow it is fearless.

SORRY

The word *sorry* is like a pain reliever;
it relieves pain.

The word, "Sorry" destroys the pride and only forgiveness restores the love.

SOWING AND REAPING

Do not be confused by what you're reaping.
Remember you sowed it. Start planting good seeds.

Anything you do whether good or bad is like sowing a seed and surely the fruit is greater than the seed.

STRENGTH

The outer tiredness produces inner strength.
The tiredness that produced produces strength.

Suffering is the beginning of strength.

STRESS

Your stress will make you progress.

STRONG-WILLED

The strong-willed takes the chance and are never afraid of losing while the skeptic blocks it with doubts and words of discouragement.

STUBBORNNESS

Stubborn people are worse than the deaf person. They hear, but never listen.

A wise dog is more teachable
than a stubborn person.

STUPIDITY

A man with good sense can be stupid if being aware of what is wrong and yet keeps insisting on doing it.

Just because you're intelligent,
doesn't mean you don't have any weakness.
But falling and indulging in to it
is stupidity.

TEMPTATION

Temptation means negative desire.
Be on guard; temptation never rests.

TEST

Test is the result of faith.

Tests don't always come in difficulty,
but sometimes in comfort.

Trials boost faith.

THE FRUIT

Pride is the father; boastfulness is the mother.
The fruit is failure.

Laziness is the father; ignorance is the mother.
The fruit is poverty.

Diligence is the father; perseverance is the mother.
The fruit is comfort.

Responsibility is the father; love is the mother.
The fruit is sacrifice.

THE GOOD SIDE AND THE BAD SIDE

We have a good side and a bad side. Our destructive weakness is the bad side. If we protect and give it reason instead of overcoming it, it will destroy others... and ourselves.

THE JERK

If you want a jerk to talk seriously,
wait for him to get lonely.

The jerk makes the king laugh.

THE SWORDS

God gave the couple swords to use to defend their
home from any destruction and harm. But instead of
using it for protection, they use it on each other.
tsk tsk

THINK BEFORE MOVE

Most of our troubles are caused by our own actions,
and blaming others is the way to escape.
Think before move.

THREE THINGS EASE PEOPLE'S MINDS

Free from guilt, free from debt,
and living in their own house.

tIME

Chase time and it will run faster. Wait for it, and you'll get bored.

Do something while waiting. It kills time.

tONGUE

Sharp mind, sharp tongue.

The tongue is small, but terrible; It is man's destroyer.

tOUGH

Tough guys need tough love.

The brat should be given lessons. Sometimes it needs to be tough teaching.

Punishment is the act of tough love.

Tough times produce tough guys.

If life is tough, be tough. What good does it bring if you complain?

How tough your battle is, is how tough you are.

TRAVELER

Life is a journey and we are the travelers. Hatred, self-pity, bitterness are all trash items of baggage and heavy loads to carry. It will steal your attention to your destination. Be wise - be focused. Leave it and keep moving forward.

TRUTH

Truth picks no one, fear no one.

It's irritating and then inspiring.

The truth will explain for you.

TWO KINDS OF THINKING

See something from nothing.
See something as nothing.
Thinking matters most.

WITHOUT JESUS

Without Jesus,
You can be happy,
But without joy.
You can be strong,
But without strength.
You can be silent,
But without peace.
You can be somebody,
But still nobody.
Without Jesus,
You can have everything,
But still have nothing.

Why Not?

If swallowing pride can get you through the challenges of life, why not?

Sit, talk, listen, and consider, why not?

Warning

The bad thing you do to others is just planting a seed to them.
The harvest of the fruit is yours.
You will feel the pain you inflicted on others.

Warrior

Disability is just a part of the great motivation a brave warrior has.

A warrior speaks about winning even in times of loss, because he sees loss as temporary.

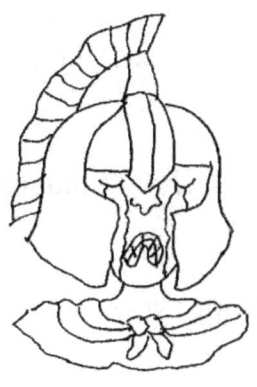

WASTEFUL PERSON

A wasteful person will not escape deficiency.

Give money to a wasteful person, and he will think of what to buy. While the economical person will think how to make it flourish.

A wasteful person and a person who doesn't know how to handle business have a common characteristic - bankruptcy.

WEAKNESS

Your weakness should be your strongest point.

Don't tell people your weakness; they might use it to mock you.

Weakness is like any substance that can make you high - it has the dosage that can make you fall.

Be aware of your weakness, your stumbling block. First it will stumble you, then it will block you on your destination.

Be vigilant about your weakness. It's your vulnerability.

Enjoy your weakness and it will become a rebellion against **GOD**.

WEARY?

A weary mind
longs for nothing,
but an ear.
A weary heart for
rest.
A weary soul for peace.
Are you weary?
Jesus has everything
you long for.

WICKEDNESS

The conscience is the guard and companion of a person. If it gets harder, he is free - free to be wicked.

The life of the wicked is like a race - race of death.

WISDOM

The fear of the Lord is the beginning of wisdom. The wisdom that will be given to you is so simple. Not that to know everything, but to distinguish right from wrong. To have sound mind and judgment.

WITHOUT PURPOSE

To live and achieve the satisfaction of your own pleasure can be measured as a life of fulfillment... and a life without purpose.

WOMAN

Women are like pictures. You can have them in clear copy if properly developed.

Women are like merchandise. In order to have one, you need to invest.

A touch of a woman makes a house a home.

WORDS

A Word is more powerful than a paragraph.

Words of encouragement are a stronghold in times of trouble.

A gentle word is more heard than a yelled one.

WORK

The secret of your peace at work lies in not complaining and ignoring people who complain against you.

When you're working, you're not creating any image, but yours. Work well, create a good image.

Be happy with your work, but do not be content.

If you are unhappy with your work, do not resign yet until you find another job or your condition will worsen.

A new employee must get along with co-workers or they will destroy him, and he ends up resigning or being fired.

Wearing your crown at work, your pride and ego will give you disadvantage.

WORRY

Avoid polluting your mind with worries, or you'll live in fear everyday.

Over thinking and worrying, what's the difference?
Nothing - both cause stress.

Worrying about everything
won't resolve anything.

WRONG LOVE

You can buy love; it works while supplies last.

Never ask for love, for it is like a ripe fruit that has no sweetness when bitten.

YOU ARE SPECIAL

Each one of us is created differently. Some are like this and some are like that. You are special in your own uniqueness, for the one who created you is the Most High God. If you put your best, your uniqueness will inspire others.

YOU ARE THE PROBLEM

If you get in trouble wherever you go, the problem is you.

Your complaint may help to root out the problem. But keep complaining, and it will turn out that you are the problem.

MIX

Follow the instructions, and you do things correctly.
Read the Bible.
Read life's instructions.

A good sleep is much better than good food.

Air in the head because of victory is like mud on a new wedding gown.

The best way to help the government is to be a good, law abiding citizen.

If working makes you tired, doing nothing makes you weak.

If generosity gives joy to some people, selfishness is to others.

Be aware of rough roads. Its roughness may rough your attitude...
stay calm.

It's ok to make mistakes,
but not the same mistake.

It's not only the storm of life that makes
a better us, but also the discipline.
It washes away our rebellion.

If there's anybody who deserves your best, it's your
family and not your friends.

Loans are like a tree. Some are fruitful,
some are not.

You need to consider the good side or you'll never
learn to appreciate.

Build a good nation by molding a good citizen.
Be good parents.

To discuss is to learn, while to argue is to prove
what you learned.

You who observe goodness, your silence will push
your observer to speak for you.

As long as your conscience is clear, don't bother
with anyone's perception towards you.

Every fall is a good start for a new beggining.

Whatever precautions you do, still you can make mistakes in an unintended way.

To a child, time is so slow. To a grown-up, time is so fast.

It's easier to go down than to reach up.

Climbing is more comfortable than falling.

Seeing what good may not come will decrease disappointment.

The given thing is of no value if not put in the heart.

Pampering a lazy person is like taking away their excitement in life.

Without dedication, diligence becomes less valuable.

Some people set higher standards than God's when it comes to forgiveness.

If you think you're wiser, your patience should be wider.

Your progress can be someone's frustration.

The fun of insensitive jokes is only suitable to a close friend. A not so close friend enjoys more flattery.

Do things one at a time. Overthinking will blow your mind.

A simple question needs a simple answer.

Warning: Avoid public humiliation...
Avoid messing with your wife.

Without sympathy, it's impossible to have love.

Worrying about normal is not normal.

Collect all small compliments. Use each as an inspiration to achieve big compliments.

People have different views to tell; lose, even and win. It's up to you what to listen to.

Explaining yourself to a one sided person is useless, for he will just use everything you say against you.

Be black in the midst of white.
Be white in the midst of black.
Make a difference.

An allusion is unpleasant to hear, but straight talk is easy to understand.

In business, everything can be disposable.

Learn to be cool; for it will hold anger longer and make you think rightly in sudden troubles.

The repetitious bad habits that are never solved will cause problems - long-lasting problems.

If the discussion turns to argument, change the topic or you'll get a fight.

Covering up one mistake only creates two mistakes.

Just do good in the present, and the future will prepare itself.

Superiority complex is only applied to inferior. It's not different from bullying; both are after weaker prey.

Some destructions are visible and avoidable... a choice.

Fear is a virus and contagious.

Even if you have a wide understanding, you still feel pain. For the mind and the heart operate differently.

Be prepared for anything, so you will not be surprised too much.

Imperfection is not an offense, but if it is used to injure others, then it becomes offensive.

Happiness will be found in contentment, but reality shows that you need to strive for necessity.

The problem with the unlearned is not ignorance. It is ignoring learning.

Your delay is the right time... in God's view.

The heart will decide who will you love, not the eyes, not the mind.

This world is really a war zone. Those who reject learning reject the best weapon.

The best weapon of ignorance - inquire.

Start to plant, and tomorrow you will reap. Start to sleep and tomorrow you will fail.

Underestimation can cause failure.

What you are today is the effect of yesterday and will affect tomorrow.

Open the door of your understanding and things can be easier.

The shame of defeat will silence your enemies.

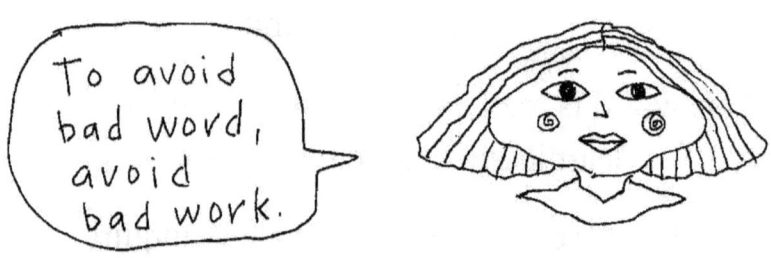

The fastest way to elevate is to step on others.

Lower your standards or be a problem.

People are more admired not by being good in adapting other cultures, but by expressing their culture wherever they are.

Rebellion is like throwing a stone in the air that falls on the head - on your head.

Backstabbing is a character that is like a bottle of medicine that contains poison.

Sometimes, when it's already near, we say, "I can't do it anymore."

Adultery is a very poisonous thing. A drop of it can ruin a strong home.

Sometimes, a desperate move becomes an act of embracing humiliation.

> After the rain, there's a beautiful rainbow.

Scaring results in anger. Diplomacy results in respect.

Heavy load gets heavier while it lasts.

There's no wild animal in a delicious snare.

We will not be known and remembered by name, but by character.

Correction is an awkward thing,
but it's a part of the solution.

Sometimes, when the heart talks,
the mind shuts up.

Every circumstance evolves learning.

Every expert begins at trying hard.

Mistake produces insight.

After grieving, keep walking.

Sometimes, the more you rush, the more it lasts.

Simplicity makes one beautiful.

Having understanding and patience enough for others means only that you are done dealing with yourself.

Idea starts everything.
It is the father of all invention.

The best way to eliminate an enemy...
reconciliation.

In God's appointed time, impossible is possible.

The listener picks up everything when the speaker gives everything away.

Different crimes often happen at night.

As long as the mind is rolling, writing never stops.

Acceptance gives you peace.

You cannot find progress in a big city. It's in your effort.

There's no pure thing to a dirty mind.

Successful people do not just use their mind, but they are also well organized and disciplined.

The more you talk, the more chance for mistakes.

One of the reasons God made you strong is, perhaps, to defend the cause of the weak.

Seeing is believing. If people see Christ in you, then they will believe you are a Christian.

In the long wait, choose to be better and not bitter.

The precious thing you could give is the thing that is precious to you.

If you want to know why it bears that fruit, dig to the roots.

A good relationship needs good communication.

Dictatorship is the thing that is vomited by all.

Stay away from people who make you feel like nobody. It will be hard for you to grow as a person.

Just do the work, and let God do the rest.

Even the bravest person feels fear.
That's human limitation.

Treat where you are as a training ground only.

Greedy means never getting full.

When you're hungry, don't mind if the food is good or not. What matters is you get full.

When you don't have anything, you have to try every good thing.

Pain is just a process of becoming smarter... Keep going

The wait is always better than being late.

Laziness, tiredness, stillness, waiting,
and resting are different from each other.
But all are doing nothing.

Risking your life in danger for the sake of
attention is really idiocy.

The loving parents denied the comfort for the sake
of their offspring.

The gathered anger that loosens may
result in violence.

A little beauty gives cheerfulness in
the midst of difficulties.

Justifying wrongdoings will result
in a crooked mind.

Be sure that your employees are being fed well
so that they will have the strength
to make you prosper.

Where you are is not your destiny.
It's up to you whether you stay or advance.

Grace applies to all. To those who have not
and to those who have.

Live your confession or be un-credible.

Hope is the appetizer of life.

Common sense is a good teacher.

Interest helps you learn fast.

Peace is immunity.

To appreciate is to motivate.

It's the rise that counts.

Exploration means discovery.

Faith sees what others cannot.

Inspiration is contagious.

Bury the past, dig for the future.

Presence is a good encouragement.

Listening is learning.

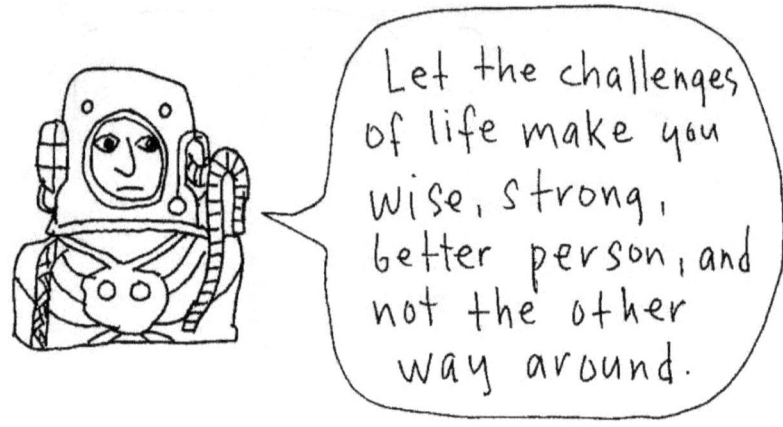

Maturity means understanding.

Cry means deeper connection.

Black signifies strength and mystery.

Lying destroys credibility.

Preparation equips all tasks.

What you are is what you attract.

Check everything before diving in.

Beware: Mouth is so powerful that it can kill a good relationship.

Today is the future for this is the day you planned yesterday... keep planning.

Sadness may lead to realization.

People come and go... be used to it.

You cannot change conviction,
but you can change perception.

Having different wives seems admirable, but actually, it is a failure.

When things start falling, maybe God is calling.

Give the person dignity and it will inspire him to be good.

The simplest form of enjoyment — laughter.

An additional responsibility proves only that you are increasing capability.

There's a good seed in you that needs cultivation to be fruitful.

If cannot live alone, learn to get along.

A little favor you gave to the least will never be forgotten.

Some people say, "Enjoy life while you are young," and time will answer, "grieve when you're old."

Progress for all starts with everyone's discipline.

Playing stupid is the most popular alibi of the people who make mistakes.

Cooperation and organization make things easy.

Credibility is in responsibility.

Wasting time from the thing that really doesn't matter is really a waste of time.

Holding hands in spite of... The secret of long-lasting relationship.

Be glad when people pull you down in any way. It's just a sign that you are moving up.

Instead of blaming, talk about the solution; blaming will just worsen the situation.

When the heart is overflowing, the mouth keeps talking.

Sleeping is one way of escaping reality.

If you think you're always right, you are wrong.

Hold your smile in front of mockers. Seeing you affected gives them pleasure.

Provocation is the father of all wars, and paying attention is the mother.

Every goal is in the matter of self-sacrifice.

Studying without learning is really a waste of time, just like going to church without changing.

People may be mad at you not because of doing bad, but for setting limitations.

Cleanliness is the beginning of a clean mind.

It's difficult to buy medicine on a sick person.

One of the good legacies is how people remember you.

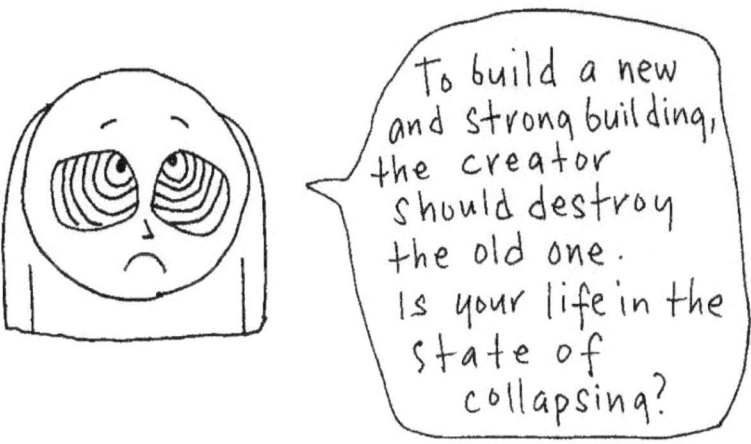

To build a new and strong building, the creator should destroy the old one. Is your life in the state of collapsing?

Get up and walk.

Let the discouragement of people encourage you more.

Vandalism is an art.
The art of anarchy.

What kind of influence do our children have when we live in anarchy?

Vandalism is the art of destruction, burden, and no care.

PEOPLE

A deaf person is better than a person who doesn't listen to explanations.

Until a man is successful, he will never be heard of.

A diligent person works even if he feels lazy. A lazy person works too, but only if he wants to.

In the mind of the arrogant, humility is cowardice and foolishness.

A person without vision is already satisfied with board and lodging.

A person who's after the praise of man ignores the humble in the midst of a gathering.

People who fear God battle weakness every day, but those who are not are enjoying it.

The worst enemy of a person is himself.

People are so eager to get to the highest point of satisfaction. Until some found out that it is the most boring place.

Better is a person whose mind is over his disability.

An adult must be already a problem solver and not a problem maker anymore.

A person who doesn't know how to persevere is easily disturbed.

People treat everything the way they value it.

A drunk person tells a lot of stories, even the most secret one.

A person who loves to ask gains learning.

A generous person will prosper.

A person who needs something is easy to command.

Even a person without good manners respects too. But he just picks.

An arrogant person never listens to explanation, because he thinks he's right.

A person who trusts God shakes, but is never uprooted.

The good and the better people vanish in bad times. But the best remains.

A patient person is a strong person.

A dangerous man is always in danger.

A snobbish person is better than a fake one.

People are stronger when angry.

People talk only when people listen.

Ignoring shuts up people's mouths.

The person who troubled you
will not leave you empty.
He will leave a valuable lesson.

People lie even if they destroy others
to save themselves.

A person who never stops asking is a tiring thing
to the giver.

The voice of the prosperous is heard even when
whispering, while the poor is already yelling,
but are still ignored.

The word of the humble is in the essence of request, while
the prosperous is on command.

The trouble maker always declares war that
brings destruction to itself at the end.

A person who lost hope often involves another.

The unkind becomes kind when sick.

The cautious still has more advantage than those
who are not.

There are still people who tell a story where they are
wrong.

Some people are wise in theory, but poor in application.

The diligent might not get rich; but surely,
he will not get hungry.

A lazy person is very kind to the diligent. It is like a plant
to him. He waters it every day then eats the fruit.

Never argue with a person who thinks he is very wise.
You'll just end up an ignorant for him.

A curious person is a potential customer.

Do not boast to a boastful person for he will treat you as a threat... a competitor.

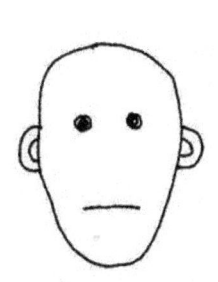

Why arguing a mentally ill person, you will not win anyway?

A beautiful face can be an image of a monster if the person inside is terrible.

Panic makes simple things very scary.

Fragrance is a gift, but it is a curse to an asthmatic.

A bed is a place of comfort, but to an insomniac, it's a place of torment.

Problematic means, everything is a big deal.

Finish what you have started. Don't be a chicken.

Do not baby a sick person for he may pamper his illness.

You need to be ambitious in order to prosper.

You can tame the tongue, but not the eyes.

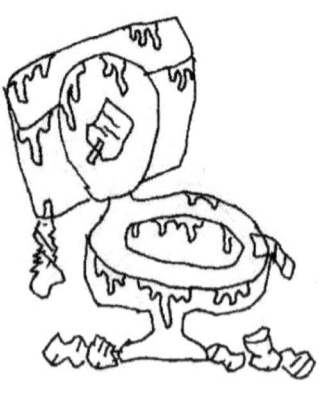

People of the city, you have the most civilized place of the world... Act like one, specially in the public restroom.

Do not confess your secret to a gossip monger. Surely it will spread out.

Who can make a man crazy? His wife. Who can make a wife crazy? Another wife.

Anarchy begins at home.

Avoid tension,
Avoid argument,
Avoid anger,

Avoid messing with your mother-in-law.

Avoid putting success in the head for it may not contain it and result in a big head.

Divorce is like bombing a building. I wish mom is not the bomber.

Where can you find a noisy woman?
In the house of an irresponsible man.

Do good,
Do bad,
Do nothing,
people say something.

When wife is working, the husband power is 50% only. When he got fired the only power left is for the house keeping.

Sometimes, it's the mouth that needs satisfaction, not the stomach.

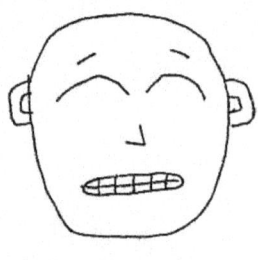

Don't mess with the person who knows your secret.

When life jokes, it's not funny.

A person without a word always promises tomorrow- for tomorrow never ends.

www.ingramcontent.com/pod-product-compliance
Lightning Source LLC
Chambersburg PA
CBHW071722040426
42446CB00011B/2181